Nails

NAILS

GARY GILDNER

University of Pittsburgh
Press

Library of Congress Cataloging in Publication Data

Gildner, Gary.
Nails.

(Pitt poetry series)
I. Title.
PS3557.I343N3   811'.5'4   74–17528
ISBN 0–8229–3293–8
ISBN 0–8229–5257–2 pbk.

Thanks are due to the editors of the following magazines for permission to reprint poems in this book: *The Above Ground Review, The American Review, The Antioch Review, Counter/Measures, Crazy Horse, fiction international, Field, Foxfire, The Great Lakes Review, Lillabulero, The Nation, New American Review, New Letters, The New Salt Creek Reader, The North American Review, Perspective, Poetry Northwest, Stone Drum*, and *Sunday Clothes*.

"The Mortician" first appeared in *The Antioch Review*. Copyright © by The Antioch Review, Inc. First published in *The Antioch Review*, Vol. 31, No. 3; reprinted by permission of the editors.

Thanks are due also to the National Endowment for the Arts for a fellowship, and to the Corporation of Yaddo.

This book is for my mother,
for my sister and brother,
and in memory of my father
who brought us all together

Contents

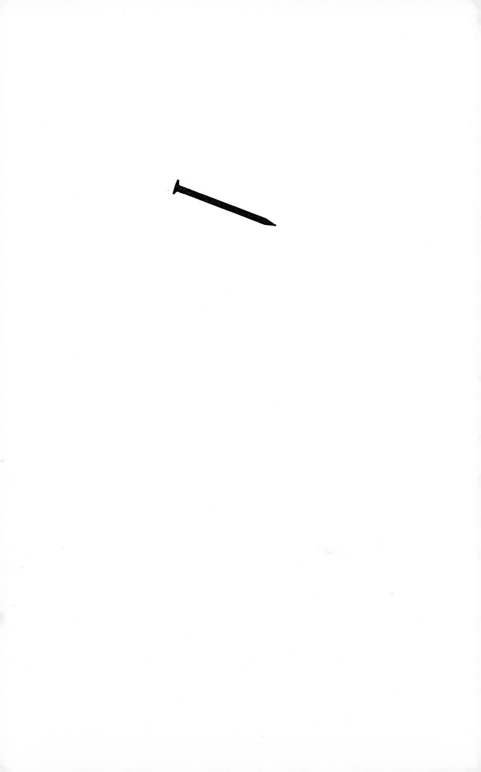

The House on Buder Street

My father found it after the war—
five rooms and two long rows of purple grapes
beside the picket fence in back
—which Eddie Hill, holding his jewels, leaped
the night we peppered a township
cruiser with bird-shot cut
from shotgun shells and stuffed in our BB rifles.

Every summer my mother made grape jelly
and Eddie, who had it down pat, polished my curve ball.
Up in his attic we gagged on rum-soaked Crooks;
he described taking a flashlight to bed
and crawling under the sheets
the nights he slept with his older half-sister.
Our houses were back to back.

The Buder Street brain was Jerry Skellinger.
He had a wing like a chicken
but could figure a Tiger's average without a stick or paper.
Once throwing darts I got him in the shoulder.
His father taught math and after school put peacocks
and roses in blocks of clear plastic.
They had a black cocker named Silly.

The night my brother was born
my father and I slept in the basement—
on Grandma's brass bed hauled down from the farm.
I was afraid of spiders
and clung to his back.
My aunt Sophie came from Detroit and steamed bottles
and made my sister and me eat everything.

I thought I'd be a doctor.
I took a kitchen knife and cut the cry
thing from my sister's doll. She screamed.
My aunt sighed Be constructive.
I filled a can with polliwogs from Miller's Pond.
I watched Shirley Fox bite her warts.
Shirley came from Arkansas; her parents hated Catholics.

When my brother could toddle he climbed
a ladder and fell on his liver.
Then he picked up hepatitis.
When he got on his feet we lit sparklers
and buried hot stones to bake potatoes.
Shirley's warts were gone, too.
She'd lifted a robin's egg and rubbed on bloody bird.

Now we needed a bigger house.
Bigger also meant better.
My mother hated the dusty unpaved street,
the soot from the coal-burning furnace;
and her fruit cellar was packed!—
she couldn't can another pickle.
Some nights my father slept in our room.

The fall my mother insisted I still needed
long underwear, I threw them at her.
My father knocked me down,
then grabbed a long-handled hammer
and began to hit the house.
The rest of us cleaned up the chips.
By winter we had a new bedroom.

In the spring Shirley's breasts appeared.
Eddie worked on my slider and Miller's Pond
was filled in to build what my father called cracker boxes;
they were painted orange and lime and raspberry sherbet.
Some of Shirley's kin from Arkansas moved in one.
They went to work for Fisher Body, like her father,
and called each other shop rats.

My sister and I attended the Catholic school—
everyone else went to public. Eddie reported
that Shirley crossed her legs in Algebra; he figured
to make All-County and carried Trojans in his wallet.
My mother counted the Baptists on the street.
My father called it harping.
Sunday drives meant looking for a lot.

After World War II

We piled in the car
& went for a ride!
My mother wore lipstick,
my father wore slippers
& the kids poked their heads
out the windows & giggled
at people kissing.
Later we stopped
at a Bo-Kay stand & punched
each other in the fuzzy back seat
while waiting for seven flavors.
Then my father lit up, my mother
blotted her lips,
and we pulled into
Country Club Lane
which went in a circle under the moon,
and we promised to behave—
and look at the dark
brick houses, the long
carpet lawns feeding little brown deer,
and the *swoosh*   *swoosh*
of sprinklers
and the colored cars, and a lady
wearing high yellow hair and holding
a little white cup,
out strolling a yellow dog
that looked back at us
until we were out of sight.

Nails

My father, his mouth full of nails,
is building my mother's dream house.

My mother is listing the grief
it cost her, & pointing out how smooth

the woodwork is. To her brothers:
well, the blacks are taking over—

& her cousins passing through from Santa Monica
swear the church is kissing ass. Ah,

a dream house draws the line on many
fronts. (St. Monica, if I remember, wed thou thee

a pagan, no? & brought him in the fold.
& when he died thou set

to work on sonny boy, old dissolute Augustine, right?
Any food in there for thought?)

Meanwhile, time to pour
the basement floor,

& the Ready Mix man plops
his concrete through the future

rec room window, *Lord*
it isn't wet enough to spread!

Just lays there like a load some giant chicken
dropped. My father, mixing figures,

says all hell will hit the fan
if our fannies do not *move*

& sets my little brother on it with the hose
while we grab hoes & shovels, Lord

I liked that part & afterwards
the lump all smooth

we drank our beer & pop
& mopped our sweat,

& talked about What Next.
The future meant:

cut the lumber square,
make the nails go straight

& things will hold.
I loved that logic, saw him prove it—

then he said we're done
& covered up the last nail's head

with wood paste;
everything was smooth.

I moved around a lot
when I left home, making stories up.

In one blockbuster there's a lady says:
"You taste like roofing nails, father."

And: "You're growing shorter!"
Terrific dialogue but not much plot.

Like building dream houses—
no one knows what you mean.

Passion Play

I am the son who steers his father's chair, his hawk
    fingers caressing a nugget of nitroglycerin

We are ten angels in two straight lines, under the eyes
    of a woman who wears a fox

We are a pair of clerics
    who wager the Pirates have all the guns

I am the one with a good nose
    I smell camel manure, sawdust, urine, sperm

I am a girl with marvelous legs, because of me
    men groan in their sleep, palm their throbbing hearts

I am a boy in spotless white bucks
    she has promised me her blood

I am a child with chalk for bones, I am tied flat
    they oil my crank, they point me in the right direction

We are the ones who twitch and shiver and drip
    our nerves are a joke

I am blind, I squeeze
    a rubber ball, I keep in shape

I am a white woman in a green sari
    my companion, the midget, crosses and recrosses his bandy legs

I am the midget
    my companion wears a dot of lipstick on her brow; I adore it

I am a housewife and mother
    the midget kicks my chair, breathes on my hair

9

I am a breadwinner
    I carry binoculars; I have a boil on my neck

I am a teacher from Kansas
    I have run away to love, to give and receive

I am a widow, I prefer dark meat, the liver
    I sew having buried my husband's genitals

I am Christ
    everyone knows my story; I am surrounded

I am Judas
    I am cursed in bars

We are the camels, we drive Pilate the fanatic
    crazy with our filth

I am Peter, I am bored to death
    denying my Master three nights a week

I am the blind man, I switch my ball from hand to hand
    anxious for the cock to crow

I am the child
    He has promised me Eternal Life

We are the lovers
    our mouths water

I am the teacher
    crush my lips

We are the clerics
    we are on vacation

I am the breadwinner
my boil has come to a head

I am the mother
I have lost a breast; my husband wipes his neck

I am the midget, I feel
spikes in my feet, I kick

I am his companion
I tried to be a Catholic

I am the son, my father says wait
your turn will come

I am the mannikin
at the Resurrection I rise, I glow

We are the hands that man the booths at the end
we hold up beads, authentic rags

We are the ones who rush
who brush away our tears, who buy

The Closet

After they opened the new church
the small cross came down
from the sanctuary in the old one
and went in a closet with odds and ends,
with bent or mateless candlesticks,
with a string of pearls a Puerto Rican
lady forced on the pastor
for taking away a sin he couldn't
figure heads or tails of, with angel hair
too ratty for the crib,
with a punctured basket-
ball, with a roll
of unused tickets to the Summer Festival
at which mothers, blushing,
hustled Sloppy Joes
and the assistant pastor rattled
dice for Lucky Strikes,
with a laminated prayer
card in Latin,
with a handout advertising
Dunn's Funeral Home,
with a pair of reading glasses,
with a ripped galosh,
with a tarnished holy-water shaker,
with a polka dot clip-on bow tie,
with a postcard showing downtown Wichita
and a scrawl saying "Hi Father! Buzz & Rita,"
with a cardboard pumpkin
and a baby's pink teething ring.

They Have Turned the Church Where I Ate God

They have turned the church where I ate God
and tried to love Him into a gym

where as an altar boy I poured water and wine
into the pastor's cup, smelling the snuff
under his lip on an empty stomach

where I kept the wafer away from my teeth
thinking I could die straight to the stars
or wherever it was He floated warm and far

where I swung the censer at Benedictions to the Virgin
praying to better my jump shot from the corner
praying to avoid the dark occasions of sin

where on Fridays in cassock and Windsor knot and flannel pants
I followed Christ to His dogwood cross
breathing a girl's skin as I passed, and another's
trying less and less to dismiss them

where I confessed my petty thefts and unclean dreams
promising never again, already knowing
I would be back flushed with desire and shame

where I stood before couples scrubbed and stiff
speaking their vows, some so hard at prayer
I doubted they could go naked, some so shiny
I knew they already did it and grinned like a fool

where I stood before caskets flanked by thick candles
handing the priest the holy water
feeling the rain trickle down to my face
hearing the worms gnaw in the satin and grinding my teeth

where once a mother ran swooning to a small white box
and refused to let go calling God a liar screaming
to blow breath back in her baby's lungs

They have turned the church where I ate God
into a gym with a stage

where sophomores cross themselves before stepping
on soapboxes for the American Legion
citizenship prize
just as I crossed myself before every crucial free throw
every dream to be good

where on Friday afternoons in the wings
janitors gather to shuffle the deck
or tell what they found in a boy's locker wrapped in foil
or in a girl's love letter composed like maidenhair

where I can imagine pimpled Hamlets
trying to catch chunky Gertrudes at lies
no one believes in except the beaming parents

They have turned the church where I ate God
and tried to love Him into a gym with a stage
where now in my thirty-fourth year I stop
and bend my knee
to that suffering and joy I lost, that play
of pure confusion at His feet.

Prayer for My Father

That gleaming boat they took the time and grief
to christen with carnations and the shakes
of holy water,
let it go.
And let the pain go with it.
Let it stay down there below the roots intact,
a tribute to the undertaker.
Let him join it.
And let my father stand
as in this photograph—
planted to his hips in current, holding up a bucketful of smelt
and beaming, as if any second he might fly!

Let him fly—
and let that blur, a child's hand that fluttered into view
when he looked up,
fly with him.

What Do the Woods Whisper?

They whisper I am wearing
a red dress, I am naked
to the waist, I am a nest
of pheasants on your heart,
I am over here,   and here,
I am nowhere to be found.

What do the woods describe?
They describe men and women,
a child finding a skunk
chewing its caught foot off,
sounds that are almost wild
coming from here,   here,
coming from nowhere.

What do the woods desire?
They desire ripe apples,
the soft depression of a woman's hip
when she reaches over
to plant a spear of grass
between your folded hands,
horses among your ribs.

The Life of the Wolf

Surrounded by tigers,
pandas, and piles
of marked-down sweat-
shirts, by blown-up gnus
chewing their cuds and clerks
huddled like pocket mice,

he presses *The Life
of the Wolf* to his coat
and trembles to own it,
to have hairy feet
and impossibly keen
hearing, and to move

mainly by moonlight.
His cousins, the coyote
and kit fox, would call him
swift, and sheep
dreaming his jaws,
dreaming his rangy legs

would swoon in their fur
at his touch.
A most faithful beast,
if the right female
pricked up the hairs on his neck
he would mate forever.

For her he would tear out
the best meat, give her silver
pups to suckle, and tackle
ranchers if the moose and caribou,
the deer and elk gave out.
On rainy nights in the den

he would treat her to rhythms:
"Delicate little dik-diks
scamper on the savannah"—
and she would roll over
rubbing his side as if lost
in the ripest flesh.

Or maybe he'd fall for a collie,
and get shot forsaking safety
in the outskirts—
and she too would get shot
going for the killer's, her owner's,
throat in revenge . . .

And they'd all die out,
as in fact they were,
unable to find a place in the country,
a place away from men
riding shotgun in low-
flying planes . . .

With only their ghosts
on the shelves,
reduced and filled
with stuffing,
with fake gray fur
and satin ribbons.

The Proposition to Go Rich

Here is a world of burgundy
too old to drink,
but I am tempted, Lord, to eat
the diamonds in her fingernail dirt
and wipe my mouth off with her smile
while we lick beneath the sheets.
"How are you, darling?" Darling whispers,
and I do not answer I am fine
dust, a crust of South America, a Greek
booze you add nothing to—
I say, "I'm spent, my teeth are busted,
and the thirst is killing, darling
—how are you?"

Prayer

Our Father we want to be happy
We want the easy instructions easy
We want You to be sensible and our children rich
We ourselves want to be sensible and rich
We don't want the poor to be poor
We want them to roll their eyes forward

And we want the animals to smile when we snap their picture
And we don't want to hear that the forests are closing up
And we don't want to hear that the water has sores
And we don't want to hear that the air is crawling

We take our dogs to the doctor
And we wash and rinse and hit the line

World without end. Amen.

The Man and the Goshawk

For two straight days
around the clock, dust
has settled on their backs
and they have shared the attic,
hollow-cheeked as lovers
who can't call it off—
the man grown stiff
in some old crushed
velvet chair his mother
left behind, the hawk
in jesses, clinging to his arm.
You'd think an artist
with a taste for veiny eyes
sat them there and bellowed:
Do not move, you're beautiful!
—and mainly they behave.
When the man's wife
hands up live blue mice
trembling in a shoe box,
she, the hawk, barely pecks at them—
you can see
her heart's not in it.
But the man does not
lose faith; he chews
another No-Doz and goes over,
once again, the book
of kings at falconry.
The thing is: he must win
the goshawk's confidence,
must wait for her to feel
free enough to fall asleep.
By tomorrow that will happen.

24

Then the next day
feed her beef heart, raw
—just enough
to make her hungry;
then he'll give her twenty
feet or so of line
and let her go
and pull her in,
and let her go
and pull her in again to meat.
Let her go, he thinks,
and pull her in;
let her go
and pull her in again to meat;
let her go
and pull her in,
let her go
and pull her in
until she loves me.

Song of the Runaway Girl

I give you the rust from my hands
I give you the salt from my lover's neck
I give you the bees from my nipples
    their twelve thousand eyes I give you
    their diligence & wrath

I give you my tongue to stop the blood
I give you my hair to dress your wounds
I give you my flight, my confusion
    under your weight
    I give you my love, my hate

Burn-out

In the vacant lot
next to Eddie's Sundries, two young bruisers

forty feet apart, in heat,
burn a baseball back and forth.

Dry, I step inside
for beer.

The cooler's empty; Eddie's widow lifts her eyes
from Maeterlinck's *Life of the Bee*—

she knuckles the sweat on her lip
and calls the Hamm's man a son of a bitch.

I nod,
she lights a Kool

and sighing returns to her page.
I leave.

Outside, the boys have moved in
a dozen feet. The game is serious,

speechless, the ball lands with an oily *smack!*
It takes me back. I remember

how red my palm got
when I caught the ball too much

in the pocket
instead of the webbing—

and once so hard in the lower gut
I urinated pink for a week.

Suddenly one boy yells "You mother!"
and makes a wild heave over the other's

head. The ball hits and cracks
the plastic PEPSI sign sticking out of Eddie's.

They scram.
Eddie's widow's face

appears behind the screen
like an engraving. I can't tell how

she feels. Then
the Hamm's man

pulls his truck up, jumps down grinning.
Eddie's widow steps outside, she's wearing

yellow bedroom slippers sporting
dandelions. Shading

her tiny eyes
with the bee book, she blinks at the street,

then at the sky.
Several seasons go by.

The Hamm's man, loading his dolly,
throws her a wolfish whistle.

But she is still blinking—trying to make sure,
I think, the sky isn't kidding,

and that her eyes are in OK,
and that the voice saying

"Save it, lard ass"
really belongs to her,

and she to us, whoever we are,
before it's time to go in.

Xmas

1. Deck the halls with git.
2. Git the halls.
3. In a gitfall, stick out your tongue.
4. Remember when gitfalls were bigger?
5. For grandmother: a warm, practical git.
6. For Bing: a white git.
7. For that man on the go: a go git.
8. Git comes in all sizes, including no-return.
9. Git is color-blind & lays down its arms.
10. Jingle git.

Around the Kitchen Table

Around the kitchen table we are never out
of shape, grinning back the skinned and bleeding
shins we picked up in our first front yards,
remembering the black and blue, the sweaty
run-ins with the nuns who always had our number,
recalling how we counted time by cornsilk
curling from our burning corners,
by the hams and sausage Grandpa strung
around the smokehouse, by the smelt
we shoveled in the car and drove all night with,
breathing stars and silos, breathing whispers
in the scarves the girls gave us, counting time
by frost and field mice, by weddings and the necks
of roosters Grandma wrung to welcome us back home
—and all the while we're talking loaves of Polish
rye are going down with butter, beer, and links
of steaming kielbasa! And everyone weeps
unable to keep his hands off the horseradish.
Then Uncle John, whose knees are pocked
with shrapnel, makes up his mind on the spot
to polka with Uncle Andy, the stiff one
who wears gartered socks. And gathered around
like this, someone always recalls a relation
burdened with more than his share of grief,
and the latest passing, the latest operation.
But always there is food on the table
and always another wedding in sight—
a beautiful cousin with red hair—
and Uncle Joe will pick up Grandma and
look! already Grandma has her glass of beer,
blushing as the young blond Polish priest
bites into his chicken next to her.

My Mother's Thirties Story

Then one night
our baby sister came along
Mr. Holson had a son named John
they lived across the road
Mom said run & tell
Mrs. Holson I
need the Doctor tell him
a confinement case
& stay there with your brothers
little Joe & John—
Big John drove a truck
before it broke
& he had four
sisters under five
Alma Thelma Grace & Mary & the whole
string of us jumped
on that truck with runny noses
Well
he had to watch us
& it's February
colder than I don't know what
moonlight on the ice I guess
& there we are like cattle chickens bags
of onions beets you name it
on our way to pick up lover's
cream & peaches
redhead

Oh my
they're cozy in the cab
so warm & rolly-eyed

& *now* where the heck's he taking us!
A little spin he says all chummy
Charlie Chaplin with his cupcake
boy we're cold & hungry
little Johnny pissed his pants
they froze on him the twins
were curled up two turnips
turning purple while the Jerk
is puffing Camels
tough guy Cagney wow
a monkey that's what you are!
what a sap
we don't know when we're lucky
now he runs a funeral parlor
bites his nails mopes in black
& dandruff like a blizzard
Anyway
he got us back
you never saw such rosy
kids we stuck
our fingers in the stove
potato soup hot sauerkraut & wieners.

California Dreaming

We're here because we're not
back there. Back there is dirt
and snow and Grandpa's grave;
we send it roses every New Year's.
Here, as Ginny says, we dream—
we've got an orange tree, boat, and pool.

Weekends we go naked in the pool
with friends and drinks; it's not
what you might think. The years,
we used to say, were killing us; we had our graves
picked out; our dreams
were filling up with dirt.

Now we mix manure and thick black dirt
for marigolds and peppers, and we dream
in slimmer, copper bodies. In a year
I'll put my figure-eight and granny knot
to work; till then we're graving
Lady Luck, who's on her blocks behind the pool.

Don't ask me what our dreams,
our long-term plans are. Years
and years ago beside my father's grave
I promised him a son who'd love the dirt
as he did—as we all did once. But farming's not
for families anymore. We ride to work in car pools.

And our son Jerry? Once or twice a year
he calls; we listen to him laugh or not
say anything for what seems hours. I have dreamt

us blind: my husband's eyes and mine are pools
of grease: we can't find Father's grave!
Jerry's on the other end, digging out his fingernail dirt.

Ginny's just the opposite—in the dreamy
middle. Which is fine. She turns fifteen next year—
lots of time to find out life's not
combing out her rats beside the pool
for Buck or Lance, or Daddy kissing dirt
from hurts, or planting ivy on her turtles' graves.

Meanwhile we go on, mixing dirt and dreams
of graves, hating all the years
we were not here, and slipping into pools.

What We Left the Farm For

Before falling asleep
we sometimes remember that salt
sprinkled on a sour apple,
that pucker,
that hairy frost
on nails poking through the frozen roof,
breathing close
under the quilts,
rubbing each other's bites
by the creek, going barefoot
in cool cellars, hooting
like an owl,
minnows
swimming inside our shadows.

Kneeling in the Snow

I pray for my uncle
who quit seeing us
beating his cancer like Tarzan,

for a woman
clawing her raw, swollen belly,
her amber tongue stuck out for dope.

I pray for my daughter beating her wings,

for my father and grandfathers
hunched like bears
under the covers,

for their women
who remember the slaughter
before the wedding.

I pray for my fear,
may we lie down together.

Touring the Hawkeye State

I saw the best parts of Iowa covered with New Jersey tea,
    partridge pea, rattlesnake master, and Culver's root,
    I saw Chief Keokuk's "X" in the county courthouse in Keokuk,
    home of John L. Lewis and Elsa Maxwell

I saw sweet William, wild rye, I saw the Iowa Watershed Divide
    running through the business district of Orient,
    I saw the outskirts of Adair and the locomotive wheel
    marking the spot where Jesse James derailed the Chicago,
    Rock Island and Pacific and knocked off engineer Rafferty
    and ran with the loot to Missouri

I saw gayfeather, blazing star, and butterfly weed,
    I saw where Henry Lott murdered Two Fingers on the banks
    of Bloody Run, where Dr. William S. Pitts, a dentist,
    wrote hymns, taught singing and practiced
    in Nashua in Chickasaw County,
    home of The Little Brown Church in the Vale,
    I saw Osage, home of Hamlin Garland

I saw the home of Iowa's only one-eyed governor, Bill Larrabee,
    and Clarinda, home of Glenn Miller,
    and Humboldt, home of Frank Gotch, who hammerlocked
    the Russian Lion Hackenschmidt for the world
    wrestling championship, and Grundy Center,
    home of Herbert Quick, author of *The Hawkeye*,
    The Invisible Woman, and others

I saw the braided rugs that Grant Wood's mother made
    from Grant's old jeans, where the *Bertrand* went down
    on her maiden voyage, taking boxes of Dr. Hostetter's
    Celebrated Stomach Bitters, and the Fairview Cemetery
    where Amelia Jenks Bloomer, of *The Lily*, lies buried,
    I saw her Turkish pantaloons

I saw the only Holstein museum in America
and Mama Ormsby Burke's neck chain and milk stool
and the west branch of the Wapsinonoc and the modest
two-room cottage that sheltered young Herbert Hoover
and Peru where the first Delicious apple tree grew
and Newton, home of Emerson Hough, author of *Mississippi
Bubble*

I saw the summit of Floyd's Bluff and the lightning-
struck obelisk south of Sioux City
near Interstate 29, the final resting place
of the bones of Sergeant Charles Floyd
who died of a busted gut under Lewis and Clark,
their only loss on the whole trip,
I saw Oskaloosa where Frederic K. Logan
composed "Over the Hills" and "Missouri Waltz"

I saw the Walnut, Turkey, Pony, Plum, and Honey creeks,
the Polecat River, Spirit Lake, the park where John Brown
drilled for Harper's Ferry, Eisenhower's Mamie's
home in Boone, the home of John "Duke" Wayne, né Marion M.
Morrison, in Winterset, Billy Sunday's mother's grave
a peg from Story County's Sewage Plant,
where Billy saw the light, where he came back
to gather souls, in Garner, after shagging flies in center
for the Chicago White Stockings

I saw ½ mile west of Orient where Henry Agard Wallace,
experimentalist and Republican, Democrat and Progressive,
breeder of chickens, strawberries, and hybrid corn
and Iowa's only U.S. vice president was born,
on a nine-acre tract of virgin Iowa prairie
in West of Orient I saw pink and white beardtongue

I saw where Jenny Lind and Tom Thumb appeared
in Stone City, where Cyphert Talley, a Baptist preacher,
was killed in the Talley or Skunk River War
in Sigourney, where the Sac-Fox council
started the Black Hawk War in Toolesboro,
where Chief Wapello and his friend General Street
are buried in the same plot along the C. B. & Q.
right-of-way in Agency

I saw the trails worn in the sod by trekking Mormons,
the Corning farm of Howard Townsend, historic communist,
blue-eyed grass and Jerusalem artichoke,
war clubs, knives, scrapers, grinders, and threshers,
hickory, basswood, hackberry, wahoo, and burr,
a Victorian parlor, a low-growing yew,
a rare folding bathtub, a belfry stocked with birds

The Physical Exam

It's like being on the brink
of falling out of love,
you still have that knot
around your gut,
& the Matron of Inventory
strides in to run
down your heart-
beat, bowels, etc.
In the end you feel like 2
for a quarter. Then
you are sent out to pee
in a bottle . . .
followed by Miss Needle
who wants to draw blood.
Since five o'clock this morning
she has been humming Barber's
"Adagio for Strings" & shows
little sign of chapping.
Her lips release the news that
your five vials will short-
ly be on their way
to Portland, & tested for no
less than 25 things.
Reduced to crabs
you undress.

The doctor arrives & peers
in your ears; he says
he had a great
BLT on toast for lunch.
Then he hits your knees,
squeezes your stomach & feels
between your toes.
You wonder what's up.
He mumbles moles, cancer—
then you know, better than you
ever knew your catechism,
that you're someone else, & dead.
You turn your head & cough.
He jabs his finger in your ass
& leaves.

You dress fast—
Miss Needle might come back,
"We need five vials for Aberdeen!"
& the Matron, maybe she'd
just as soon declare a total loss—

On the street you feel light.
Some kids are playing basketball.
You skip, suck air,
recall the night you scored
your forty points
& creamed those fairies from St. Agnes.

Meeting My Best Friend from the Eighth Grade

He says when he comes in a bar
after beating Wyoming, say,
there's something like fur in the air
and people don't see him, they see a bear.

My best friend from the eighth grade is a coach.
He wants to Go Go Go Go—
He wants to Get There!—and gives me a punch.
His wife, in lime slacks, curls on the couch.

I ask him where
and thinking it over he pounds his palm; his eyes stare.
His wife passes peanuts, teases
his touchy hair.

He says never mind
and changes the subject to button-hooks, quick dives
—old numbers in our pimples we were famous for.
Nineteen years go by; he calls it a crime.

His wife cracks two more Buds, stretches, calls it
a night; we hear the door click.
Flushed, he flicks on the television . . .
We bend our beer cans like dummies, and sit.

After an All-Night Cackle with Sloth & Co.
I Enter the Mansion & Greet the Dawn

& three baby barn swallows
are being fed on the wing
on the lip of the rain
gutter next to my bathroom window.
There they squat, 1—2—3
little gentlemen dandies.
wrapped in their capes,
their necks tucked in
as if nobody loved them.
—Not true! here comes Momma
with a beakful of bug mush
& all three perk into *me-me-me!*
while flapping the air pizzicato!
Ah, the gent on the left gets it quick,
good for him, good for Momma—
& off she flits for another scoop
& they settle down.
          Dog-fashion
they scratch their heads,
pick in their slick blue
tails for appetizers,
snub a dizzy wasp . . .
Quietly, I take this moment to leak
wishing I too were starting
the day so fresh, & could flap
for something plucked
alive in mid-air, in love,
& drop my chalky crap, my gnats & flies,
in the gutter with such distinction.

45

The Wake on Goose River, North Dakota

At my uncle Jimmy Lynch's wake
we were everyone except tight Grandma
working loose to drink
the good dead man to earth,

when Grandma spilled the beans
to God, i.e. aloud she squeezed
her beads to save us from dam-
nation on this dark, queer night.

What brought the trouble up
was Jimmy's plane & Heaven;
or, our joke to buzz the saints did
rage with Grandma's recipe for Bliss.

Alas, she went to bed & we without
a leg to pull took up the Piper Cub.
Three facts amazed us:
1. the ground below was Climax, Minnesota

2. we scooped the loop & heaved our guts &
3. we landed.
At which point we drank our health
& hoped we scared the Devil shitless.

The Mortician

Hates all nationalities
especially the wailing, fainting Italians
who rise from their bouts of sorrow
and sniff their noses
at his cookies.

The Irish, the black, the Bohunk and fallen-
away Jews—they crowd around the dead
like old dead neighborhoods, and spit
and wipe their snot
like squatters.

Alive they're all alike, they're dumb,
and smell to hell. But passed away
at least they're drained
and, if smashed or shotgunned,
reconstructed.

Nobody knows how bad the living are
until he serves one up
who can't put on a thing
that is and isn't his,
and that's what drives them crazy.

The Vigil

You too can sit under your own fig tree
indoors, *eat 2 crops of delicious figs*
a year and raise something uncommonly
beautiful . . .
—from an advertisement
for a Revelation Fig Tree

We are sitting indoors this year
under the fig tree behind the piano,
waiting for a sign, growing thinner and thinner.

Our lives are common, only our clothes which glow
like roseate spoonbills,
like strawberry rashes,
are lovely to look at.

Once in a blue moon
someone will flutter with uncommon beauty,
"I am gay as a Monarch rocking away, rocking away
on a timothy stem . . ."

But exuberance soon dies, and the bitter ask
Why are there no golden bells from Chungshou?
no spinning damsels that train on drops of honey?
no crickets that kick like mules in pottery jars . . . ?

The witty say, We have sent letters on shed leaves
to the late, great W. H. Hudson
and to the late, great Saul of Tarsus
demanding our spondulix back . . .

While the sober sit and wonder, saying nothing
to disturb the rest of us
who pinch our cheeks to bring the color out.

Lead Us

All week I have been tearing up my house,
pulling off plaster in puffs of chalk dust,
clawing at floorboards, at furry lath
between which tufts of old gray insulation ooze
as if from the side of a suffering sheep.
Maybe hundreds of animals are caught behind the walls.
Maybe a bull moose driven from its new wet calf.
Maybe a small black duck whose song sticks in its throat.
Maybe a rabid fox who will lead us into the hills.

My Neighbor

is showing my daughter
his new can of Mace
his double locks
his baseball bat
his chunky face
all smiles when
our dogs romp over
"jaws" he whispers
"damage" "throat"
and swooning pats
her little head.

The Coyote's Song

It's not their lambs I love
that make them bitch and bait
their traps and cock their guns,
it's my song of loneliness,
my cry to couple under snow—

It's the mouse I play with
just before I eat her,
it's the cricket, squirrel, fat
tobacco-squirting grasshopper
and insulation wire I swallow—

It's the moon I lick,
my rhythms with the smitten,
it's the way I kiss, my autograph,
it's my freedom in an open burrow
and afterwards my belly laugh.

Goodbye

The radio preacher said don't ask him
how they shot rockets to the moon,
far as he knew they pushed a button
and a little man with a mighty big foot
kicked till the Lord wouldn't have it.
And don't ask him nothing about the theory
of relativity or anything so fancy,
far as he knew people just made it up
like they do most things that break
or go crazy. And please don't ask him how it is
God's green ball of plenty keeps
rolling and rolling, and how he himself
keeps rolling and rolling, and you, brother,
how do you keep rolling and rolling . . . ?
And I wondered about that all the way
to Waterloo, and wondered again later
after you got out and started to wave goodbye
and didn't and didn't look back,
and I remembered the time I almost succeeded
counting the fine, almost white hairs on your neck.

Poem

Finally
I will come to this:
I will take my hands
from the body that warms me,
that I have warmed
and warmed again—
and then, lying very still and
feeling the heart pump away,
I will fold them.

Final Exam

1. Why did the last bird leave?

2. If you had forty nights in the desert,
   a basket of fish all staring into space,
   and a host of solid knucklebones,
   who would you feed first?
   who would you feed last?

3. Who are the "higher minds" in line 90?
   If you do not remember line 90
   make up your own—time is money.

4. List your (   ) in the order of their (   ).

5. Is your (   ) locked?

6. Who do you love?
   Whom do you love?
   How much difference does it make, if any?

7. Discuss the simplicity of question 6.

8. Is the descriptive section organized?

9. Looking back, what did the last bird look like?

10. Be brief.

Dreams

She whispers my dreams
need to rise like bubbles,
like the bubbles a fish
sends up when it's lost
in thought. I'm caught—
I can't resist her

freckles and we kiss.
We pick out honey, bread,
we spend the summer at my place.
Oh it all works out! We pool
our dimes for Tide and
dry our underwear together.

We watch the Angels split
against the Brewers, buy a
Shostakovitch, oh we slip
inside a church and hear
each other's childhoods,
and summer's over.

Fall comes on, we fall
in love, and then it's Christmas!,
January . . . March
bites us through our mackinaws.
We thaw,
we say our vows,

we name our dances
after children, after work
we walk around the block

and greet our neighbors;
one by one they make the evening
paper, leaving tiny nest eggs

to a favorite bird or cat.
Something's funny,
something's splitting in our sides.
We lie down by the lake
and close our eyes;
our dreams are falling,
breaking on the water like applause.

That Summer

That summer at the lake
when the malemute babies
nuzzled their bones
under the cabin's floor;
when Cyrus and Meeno
stayed up late to watch
a moth weave the screen
then each other,
taking days to blink;
when the patient waves
nudged the alewives
to shore, and a startled possum
flicked his pink paws at us;
when the path we took
on our morning walk
sparkled with tracks
and our feet and knees
and then our backs
and tongues got wet
there was nothing,
not one thing
under the sun or moon
or those sweet cedar boughs
that could touch us.

Tongue River Psalm

This is Tongue River, where lovers lie down,
where they bless the fox licking its fur in the bush,
where they play the rabbit's musical bones,
where they rattle two pebbles to praise the moon.

Around the Horn

New Year's Eve

Eddie's on the mound
bearing down,
& I'm at shortstop, spitting in my pocket!
—We're the twelve-and-under champs so cocky in our jocks
it hurts . . .

God damn it Jack
that skinny kid at second's white
from drowning. Butch
in right
caught polio—they drove a nail deep
into his quick good knee
to slow the bone,

& Eddie packs a gun for blacks . . .

A little compensation, Captain,
half the field tilts . . .

Where's my girl who squirmed
in roomie's Buick
over Easter break?

My sister snug in rabbit?
—while beaming me wore Father's watch!

It's midnight
& I won't grow up—
I'm Teacher's blended pet,
crocked & cold . . .

I need sweet Judy's coat of arms,
her baby breasts . . .

That midget grinning in the hole is dead.

Sonnet

If I stood on the roof of the Republic
Insurance Company, in Des Moines, and stretched
I wonder, could I see the sun settle down
on Audubon, Iowa?

If I stood in the center of Audubon
and waved my arms like a madman
I wonder, would it disturb the birds
in Bellevue, Nebraska?

In Michigan's upper peninsula
the ore docks peeling off Lake Superior
are four stories high—

in winter a young girl's hands
are chapped and broken as this tongue—
and what I want keeps jumping off the end.

Spring Morning in Northern Michigan

These chilled pickled beets dripping long thin strips
of onions, the juice
making a pool, my face
an Indian's . . .

I am taking my time peeling
the shell
from a hard-boiled egg
that waited all night in the icebox

for now: for you
waking slowly
stretching
long bare arms, the sun

melting snow
down the sides of my house,
my eaves, singing,

to be
surrounded by skin

until I can't   stand another minute.

PITT POETRY SERIES

C O L O P H O N

The typeface in this book is Times Roman, first cut for the London *Times* as a newspaper face. Although it has never achieved popularity in this country with newspapers, it has become much used in books and magazines. Its classic roman capitals, sharp serifs, and large x-height contribute to its distinctive look and high legibility. The Linotype version is used here, and the book was printed by Heritage Printers, Inc., directly from the type which was then remelted. The design is by Gary Gore.